# Polaroids - Life in Snapshots

Shivangi Jain

BookLeaf Publishing

India | USA | UK

Presentation by *BookLeaf Publishing*

Web: www.bookleafpub.com

E-mail: info@bookleafpub.com


ISBN: 9789360949037

First edition 2024

*To Ranu Mama, love always*

# ACKNOWLEDGEMENT

When we are doing life, we hardly ever notice who all are doing it with us and above all for us without even telling.

I would like to start with the source of my life, my parents without whom everything is meaningless. All that I am is a result of all that they are and more. My brother, who has always rejoiced in my achievements more than me, no matter how big or small they are. The new entrants in my life, my Bhabhi (sister-in-law) and the queen of our hearts, my niece, Dhriti, your smiles give me the strength to keep moving ahead.

I cannot even begin to express my gratitude towards all my friends who have supported me, believed in me, cheered for me, tolerated me and gone along with my crazy ideas all this while. A special thanks to the one miles away, Prashant,  who unknowingly sponsored this journey for me! Heartiest gratitude to Rashi and Amrita who gladly agreed to be the first readers and reviewers of Polaroids.

Lastly, I would like to thank everyone who has had a deep meaningful conversation with me on my journey so far, all my well-wishers, my cheerleaders, and my silent supporters. Thank you all for keeping me strong and true to myself!

# PREFACE

Hey there, so we finally meet! I have waited for this moment for so long. I have dreamt of meeting my readers and talking to them so many times. This may be a one-sided conversation but in essence, I hope for you to find in here, a sign from the universe delivered to you by the means of my pen. I hope you feel heard, seen and find the courage to follow your dreams, to confess your love, to walk away from places where you aren't valued enough, to love with all your heart even if it gets broken sometimes, to be able to protect your kind soul, to tap into your inner strength and unleash your power. For this world is going to bring you down in so many ways, by telling you what's good for you, what you should and should not be, weigh you on the scales of gender roles and whatnot. I hope in those times, you turn to these verses and fall in love with yourself all over again!

Happy reading (:

# TABLE OF CONTENTS

# One with the nature

# Ode to an artist

Artists are true magicians
Unlike the ones on stage
With a well-practiced act
They know to appear and disappear
To magnify and intensify

And it's not just a trick, it's for real
Intuition is their best friend
And they choose to listen to it
To gather all the powers they have
To unlock and unleash each level upgrade

And you know what, they can tell
They can tell a mask from real
True from fake
And if the actor hasn't yet embodied the act
An artist can discount it to its last thread

If you ever get to see their perspective
You will be perplexed by the beauty in mess
Oh well yeah, when one can X-ray as well
There is bound to be chaos

Artists my friend are the originals
They are the creators
They are thinkers, pure and true

They are the drivers of revolution
We all so dearly need

Best of the non-conformist lot
Worst of the socially acceptable sorts
They are not the moons wandering our galaxy
They are the sun brought down to us by a
magical conspiracy

Only if we choose to stick around
We will see life flourish in us
We will know love
We will know compassion
We will know what genuine is like!

# Unexplored - it's all yours

I wonder why people get bored
When there are oceans unexplored
We have a lifetime of opportunities
Hidden beneath the burden of duties

All are destined to climb up high
All you need is to rise and try
Don't narrow down your horizons
Have faith and build your cyphers
Get the key, decode the clues
Don't wait up, nothing's coming from the blues

All that's real, that makes sense is alive
Just find yourself a force to drive
Round about it all goes
You better watch your toes
Don't think, just concentrate
Soon you will realize it's you who paints your
fate

Unstoppable is what you have to be
Experiments are what it will take to be
Words will make the swords to rattle
Work is quoted to overthrow the battle

Fall in love with the bruises, that you will
definitely have to
Boost up, it's better to fall than trying not to,
Invest in whatever life demands
Listen and follow thy commands

Don't get attached too much
Everything's planned to get detached as such
Listen to the artist that you have within
We have the onus to make this world a better
place to live in

Call for the day is to nonfictionalise your worth
It's either now or never, coz there's going to be
no rebirth
Buckle your shoes and get going
Initialize, it's even harder to lead a life that's not
fueled for living!

# Water

Water oh water what should I write about you?
You are so versatile that it makes me want to be
you
You manage to pass through even the slightest
cracks
A dream come true for a traveler on a deserted
stretch

You bring peace and calm to everyone around
But I have sometimes known you destruct what
surrounds
I come from you and one day I will sink back in
Till the time comes,
I hope we stay the keepers of each other's sins

I turn to you when am confused
You have helped me find myself more times
than I can count
You give me strength
You give me solace
Oh, the keeper of human race
Do you ever feel betrayed?

The thing is,
All of us love you
But most of us don't know how to love the best

So, we offer you prayers
And yet discharge our waste in
We love to admire you
And yet we will trade your respect in our favor

Maybe we are just a fan of tough love
And tough love is all that we know
But neither that's a justification of our
selfishness
Nor is this purely a review of you

It's more of a comment on me
For I don't know what I have done
To experience and live through
Your unconditional ecstasy

# Nurturing nature

From the hustle and bustle of cities
To the rustling of leaves
From the scorching sun rays
To the freezing waves
From the upcoming kinks
To the soothing winds
It all did change

Everything's nothing but strange
You open your eyes and love your life
You say you are thankful
You are thankful for everything that ever
happened

Junctions remain where they are
Destinations keep on drifting hour by hour
You fall in love with the traveler in you
The thinker in you
The photographer in you
You fall in love with the artist in you

You question yourself turning back
You wonder why that is?
You love your family, your home, and your
friends

But you start falling in love with yourself all
over again
You have been seeking acceptance throughout
your life
You have been looking at the wrong place you
realize
The rocks, the winds, the mountains, the trees,
the clouds and the beautifully sun-kissed flowers
all embrace you at once
And nothing but the loving nature, makes your
heart skip a beat for once (:

# One breath – A Covid story

A pile of rubbles
A heap of sand
Weighing in

Yesterday it was him
Today it's her
Every day it's a new name
A new list, a new number

There are far too many
More than you can comprehend
And how so
When we don't know
If it's our fate
Or one calculated step

Bullets faced
Holes remain
They didn't kill me just yet
Only to leave me broken
They didn't poison me
Only to let me count down

I try and breathe
But it's suffocating
I shout but there's no one to respond

I gasp
And I see one take its last
Bad times to be alive
What a struggle to survive
Me and mine
What else do I know

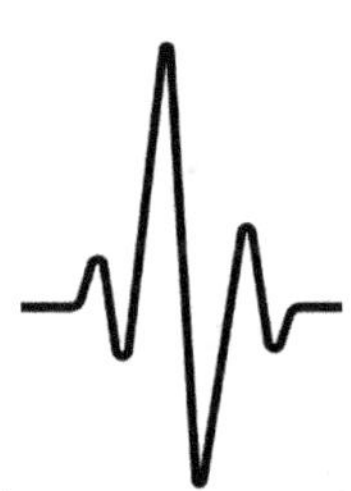

I saw you
You were crying the other night
Normally I would have asked
But I am exhausted now

For the sand is not just weighing me down
It's seeping in, it's settling
I find it hard to get up
And to get going

But I was raised to be strong
By a generation who gave
Lessons to live for others
To keep going when the going gets most difficult

So, before I lose
To the last long breath
I am here
Am holding up
One long breath at a time!

# Inanimate wisdom

# Red – A soliloquy

They went to war
They fought for their own selfish cause
They got scarred
They lost their skin
They did what they wanted to
But blamed ME for being there

Every single time they despised me
I bled
I bled for it wasn't my fault
They cut open each other and I was forced to
rush out
They made me leave my home and so I bled

They didn't like what she said
They didn't want her to come across as a winner
So, they held her prisoner
To the venom that poured out of their mouths
They raised their voice
They blew their brains out on her
And she hated ME
She started fearing me
Because I was made to captivate her
By the flush on their face and their demonic eyes
But what was my fault?
I didn't want to scare her

I didn't want her to hate me
And so I bled
For every time she saw me
She would run away
She would hide in her cocoon all scared by my
sight

But you know
Sometimes
Some people
They do not hate me
They might not love me
But they do not hate me
I like it when they do so

When someone somewhere showers them with
rose petals
When a lady decorates me on her forehead and
feels happy about it
When they associate their God with me
When they wear me on every holy occasion
When they build their world with me, pilling me
up brick by brick
When they are happy to bleed, to bring a new
character into the scene
When she gets all dolled up and her cheeks
blush to reveal the beauty of her soul

In these times I do not bleed
Because they don't deject me, for once, they are
happy to see me
For in the end, I bloom their lives up with the
showers of love

# GPS – A soliloquy

I reroute
When I see you panic on seeing the red
I reroute
I do it to increase the blue
For I don't like to see you sweat

I know you have a long day ahead
Probably a celebration to be a part of
For which you are already running late
I like to reassure you
I will tell you that you are on the best route
possible
Despite the congestion ahead

You are doing your best in the moment
I don't like to see you double guess yourself
Because when you do, you take turns
And then, I must reroute

I know you are not the best at seeing the silver
lining
Especially when the stakes are high
I don't want you to worry
At least not to get the directions right

I do leave it to you to make the judgment call
For I also like to play it safe
I have heard you curse me at times
And to tell you
I am not a fan of it
Sometimes when you are too angry at me
I see you seek outside assistance
That does hurt me

But as long as you get what you need
Reach where you have to be
And are safe
I am content

I will not lie to you
But while we are at it
Let's get it straight
I like to be by your side
No matter if you have the time to spare
Or you are on a sprint
I like to be there

I don't ask much from you
Just trust me and I will walk the road with you
till the end
I will be there at the destination with you
And yet again to explore anew

Don't be scared to take a not so fancy road
I like to, and I will do it with you
I will reroute
No matter the path
No matter the obstructions
And no matter the missed turns
I will find out the U-turns
And I promise, I will get you home (:

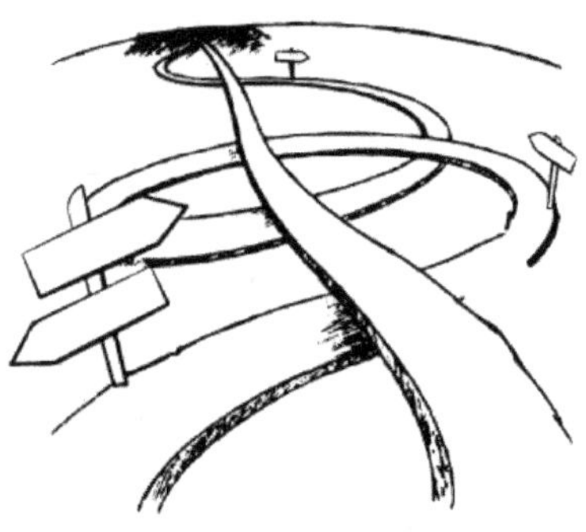

# Fridge – A soliloquy

What are you looking at lady?
I still have all that you stuffed in me yesterday

Okay, you look pretty clueless
Here, let me help you
On the top shelf, you have some peas, curd and
chutney
And

Remember a few months back you decided to
eat healthy
Yes, that thing that you see peeking from behind
The white-orange box
It's the expired yogurt that you bought then
Here's an idea, why don't you throw it out?
No?

Okay then I will keep storing it for you
Till the day you finally decide to declutter me

Just saying though
If you do it soon
I will have space for you to store more delicacies

Oh yes, how can I forget
My freezer is going through a brain freeze right
now
You see that button on the right side
Use it
Defrost me
We don't know, what treasures you might find
buried underneath

Hey hey, okay
I will stop complaining
Don't close me yet
Grab something, anything
Juice?
Chocolate?
Yogurt? No no, not that
Okay some water at least
The veggies, how about a salad?
No…

Please don't give up
I have everything you need, right here
If you would just get a little creative and pay
attention to the insides
You won't have to go searching outside

Okay
Later then…
I have faith in you

Someday, you will listen to me
Until then, I will patiently wait here for you
We have got this!

# Art-ificial

A world full of advancements
A world moving forward
Or is it really?
Maybe it's moving all but backwards?

Maze after maze
Cage after cage
Replacing the humane race
For first it was IoT then ML
Or AR, AI, VR, don't know which came after
the other
There are so many realities today
Wonder which one is real at the end of the day?

We are online
We are generating ideas
In the pursuit of becoming artificially intelligent
Are we losing our basic humane sense?

Today we fly high at the hands of our creations
Exploring the key to survive life's everyday
renditions
When all we see is virtual intelligence
And visible numbness
How are we to uphold our meaningful presence?

Maybe the future will unfold itself
And show us the way
Shedding light on "to be" and "not to be"
In the meantime,
Let's keep our real ones close
And virtual ones closer
Who is to say
Maybe they are after all our savior waiting for
exposure (:

# Pillow talk

"We have been through so much together
I have seen you laugh
I have seen you cry
I have seen you lay awake on restless nights

I served as your weapon, when you wanted to
fight
Your support, on long working nights
You hit me when you were angry
Hugged me when you felt a little too lonely

And now that we have braved through all the
seasons together
You want to trade me in for a new and fresh
variant!
Did you expect me to just leave without a fight?
Or you forgot those numerous peaceful nights?"

Ahh… only if I knew you would make such a
big scene
I never would have decided to part ways with
you
Oh, dear pillow of mine,
If I keep you put
Can we reserve the drama for me, in our future
nights?

# The color story

Tipi tipi top, what color you are…
I am white
The white that you see after the rain clouds
subside
The white of a sailor's uniform
The white of enlightenment through knowledge
The one of sorrow, surrounding a widow's pain
The white of a pearl that radiates the more it
ages
The white of peace, calm and tranquility
The white that splits into a rainbow

Tipi tipi top, what color you are…
I am red
The red of love and passion
The red of a bride's fashion
The red at the heart of vengeance
The red that smells of roses
The red of blood on a newborn baby
The one of a mother's worry
The red of a blush that makes you all tingly

Tipi tipi top, what color you are…
I am green
The green of grass
The green of moss

The green that encompasses nature and nurtures
us within
The green of nutrition and health
The green of signals that tells you to keep
moving ahead
The one that blesses a farmer's harvest
The green of flags that tells you it's worth it

Tipi tipi top, what color you are…
I am blue
The blue of the ocean
The blue of a clear sky
The blue of indigo and our Nation's pride
The blue disguised to be a boy's identity
The one that we feel after a long vacation
The blue of feeling low and disconnected
The one of a dancing peacock's poise

Tipi tipi top, what color you are…
I am yellow
The yellow of daisies and sunflowers
The yellow of sunshine
The one of warmth from the sun
The yellow of our mom's jewelry
The yellow of our mental well-being
The yellow of a youthful cheer
The yellow of unparalleled energies
The one that showers you whole and leaves you
happy

Tipi tipi top, what color you are…
I am black
The black of diamonds, rare and precious
The black of hearts with all true but outrageous
The black of a tree's cooling shade
The black of an unfamiliar shadow
The one of a moonless night, where the stars
guide you home
The one that's a necessary absence
So, all of us can value the presence

Tipi tipi top, what color you are…

# unCommon strength

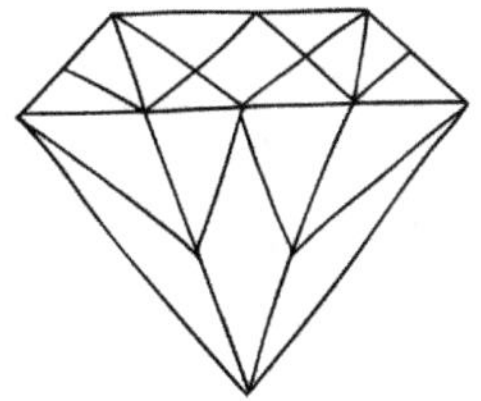

# Stories of today

You must have read about battles fought
Lives lost and nations won
Borders invaded and cultures exchanged
Businesses inherited and trades expanded

You must have read of mighty kings and wise
queens
Pretty princesses woke by charming princes
Knights in shining armors and saviors on white
horses
Of breakthrough inventions changing the course
Of pen being mightier than sword

But I
I want to tell you stories of today
Of silent cries and magnified showcase
Of everything afloat and emptiness within
Of arguments polarized
Convenient to fool us to sleep
When there's a war going on in the shades

I want to tell you how the world of today has
changed
So much so, that the lessons of history are
reduced to award-winning fiction

I want to tell you how the women of today are
still fighting to be considered equal and treated
with respect
How men even today can't cry when distressed

I want to tell you how we have advanced and yet
managed a blow below the belt
How we have become comfortable with an
overtly skewed scale
For there are weights
Weights attached to everything we say, we see,
we do
Weights that we don't remember unlocking on
our mission to live free

Yes, I want to tell you stories of today
How heartbreaks are not considered painful
anymore
How we take pride in being strong
And not discussing what's wrong

I want to tell you stories of today's society
That meets more on social media than
one-on-one socially
I want to tell you how we have set ourselves in
factory mode
Following a template without a question of who,
what, when, and why
Well of course!

I want to tell you stories of today
Of warriors found between you and me
Of common men doing highly uncommon deeds
Trying to strike a balance between what's wrong
and what's utterly distasteful
Adding color, music and warmth
When all we are served is cold and stale

I want to let you in on a little secret
A vision for tomorrow based on today
We will pass on a legacy half empty, half fake
Covered with poses hiding behind filters of all
shades
To build a world even more confused and lost
Of living deads
Of hopeless heads

I want to tell you that we can still WIN this
Wonder how, when we have so many dents to
fix?

Pick up one and start today
Pick up close and turn off that device in your
hand
Pay attention to a world crying for help
For you are the only force that can set you in
motion

You are the only force that can help others shift a little over!

# Prisoners of the dark

There's a world that wakes up at night
A world that doesn't see the daylight
Amidst those finding it difficult to breathe
Some don't know how for themselves preach

In the pursuit to wear sparkle and shine
Time and again they stretch and break their
spine
Love for them is a wishful luxury
For all they are told is to make love and hurry

Rooting for the third, day after the other
Living for the herd night after night
World for them is limited to a stick and hole
I wonder can they ever feel whole?

Where do they come from?
What's their sunshine?
If only someone, somewhere, sometime asks
They might build a claim on their very own
stride!

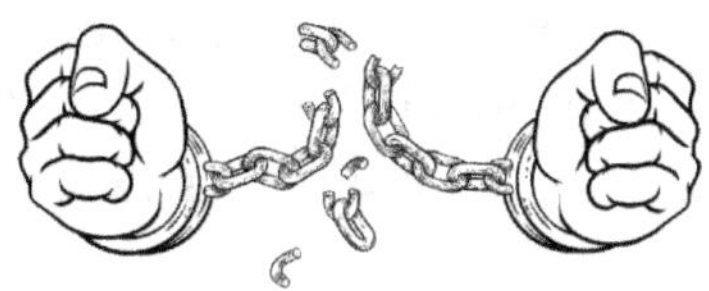

# You are you

You have so much in yourself that you don't
know of
You are more than you give yourself credit for

You are the only host to imaginations
A deep sea of unrealized passions
A room full of undiscovered emotions
A body full of soulful notions

You are you
You are more than a name and gender
You are not defined by your age and banter
You are a bundle of hidden verses waiting to be
known
You are sworn to the nightlight thrown

You are remembered in someone's worship
You are more than worried about censorship
You are not born to follow thy lead
You are here to create a news feed

You are you
You have eyes to not only see but perceive
You have ears to not only listen but understand
You have a voice not just to make noise but
speak

You are a structure of flesh and blood,
Not only to decorate but to be comfortable in
You are what you want to be
You are a heartwarming melody

You are you
You are a friend, a lover, and someone's dream
come true
You are a parent, a guardian, and a superhero to
you know who
You are a teacher, a mentor, and the creator's
hand, making something new
Above all, you are you

You are human and you have the freedom to
start anew
You are made up of ice and blue
You are the fire you fuel
You are the wilderness
You are what you nurture
You are more than what you wear
You are what's beneath the deceiving, you are
rare

You are an inspiration
You give someone hope
You are the kindle behind a million thoughts
You make a difference

You are all of you and none of what they want
you to
Just remember, you are you
Pure and new
Scarred but brewed
And you are not just beautiful
You are a piece of art that still shines in the
darkest of hours

Just don't give up so soon
If not one, then two, if not two then three
The roads you can walk are not A to Z
You have one to infinity to walk and reroute
You can do more than you give yourself credit
for
You are you
And you are undefeatable by the worst of storms
waiting for you!

# She is strong

She was strong
They said no it's wrong
Throughout the day with her usual course
*No, it cannot be usual of course*

Her smile was the jewel she carried
*We will make sure it is deep down buried*
Her independence was her life
*How could we let it survive*
Fear she thought was for the weak
*Don't worry baby we will show your leaks*
She was happy and content
*Get ready for a forever dent*

"I cannot tell how horrifying it was,
I could see the blood welling up in their eyes
There they came and did as they said
They made me believe even I was one of the
weaks
Then they gave me a gift for ever,
A fear that will leave me never ever"

Life for her, never will revive to normal
Congratulations, we are claimed animals!
For the first time,
Her wings were down

Her sky was brown
She put down her crown
She could not get over the disturbing frown

For the last time,
She thought she was a lady
She heard the heartwarming melody
She smiled wholeheartedly
She loved unconditionally

But then it occurred to her
It is the pussy that purrs
She was a lioness she knew
She had been fighting forever, this was nothing
new

Some chapters are not meant to be revised
Some lessons just need to be realized
If it's she, it's her life
Nobody gave you the remote to shuffle the
channels otherwise

The dark had been her happiness giver
Now every time it will make her shiver
The dice has rolled
And the present arrived
Yes, she is strong
Nobody in the world can turn it wrong!

*Conditions applied

# Concrete men in a concrete jungle

Dressed up outside
Choked up inside
With an outfit oh so loud
Hiding the insides filled with doubts

Hi there, this is Shivangi
And I present to you the "Concrete Jungle"
Once upon a time there lived a human species
Evolved from ages of hardship
Tracing footsteps back to their forefathers
Yet, leaving no hope for their grandsons and
granddaughters

Oh sorry, was that too harsh?
Maybe, if I don't say what I want to
Sugarcoat it with a generally acceptable
expression
Keep suffering within
And say, "All is good" with a high held up chin
It would look better

Perhaps then we will continue to create a world
anew

A world full of concrete men in a concrete
jungle
A world quite high on pretense
Somewhat low on substance

But that's okay
It's a world full of friends
Friends who tag you all day long
Friends who you may not recognize if you meet
them at all

Wait, before we get all too cynical
Let me introduce you to the tools of a world so
whimsical
With a round of applause let's welcome, "the
antisocial media"
Umm my bad, "the social media"

Wonder what it is?
It is this place… umm not quite
It is this medium… nay even that's not right
So basically, it's this thing that is used by the
concrete jungle species
To stay connected with one another
The concrete men have friends on it… in it…
yeah you get it
An average of about 400-500 to say the least
Isn't that nice, having so many friends to talk to?

The concrete jungle seems to be one happy place
then

People are seen tagging each other all day long
Saying they are "there" to keep everyone strong
But sometimes I wonder, where is this "there"
It's hardly visible to the naked eye
Because in the concrete jungle my friend,
Concrete men are friends with concrete men

Like the seven wonders of the world
Mentioned together
Tagged with one other
Physically apart
And emotionally discharged!
So yeah, I will call it a wrap now
This was Shivangi
Introducing to you, for the very first time
Concrete men in a concrete jungle
*"Don't forget to tag me if you quote me"*

# Freedom is two-letter word away

I want to be a cricketer
Let me go out and play
NO sit and study, do your homework
Girls belonging to good families don't play on
roads
So, she sat down, stayed in and completed her
homework

I want to study literature
Let me pursue my interest
NO literature is no good
What will you do, become a teacher?
Take up something that has scope
He didn't want to argue with his people
So, he took up something more conventional
Having ample backups

I want to be a writer
I want to discover my true self
Let me stay alone for a while
NO I don't understand
Why do you want to stay alone, it's not safe
Tired of making them understand, she just
stayed quiet this time

After a lifetime of NO
She didn't want to waste her strength on
explanations anymore

That girl who was asked to stay in, is still there
Hiding behind her books, refusing to show up,
That guy still questions his decisions
Isn't it too unconventional?
What would I do if this doesn't work out?
Do I have a backup?
The wishful writer is so tired of explaining
herself
That she is on her way to take a final step!

For every single time they said NO
A part of them got silenced within
They could not be, what they should have been
Only if they were left free
To live their own reality!

# A kid was once told

"Don't act like a kid"
A kid was once told
"This doesn't concern you,
you are not even that old"
A kid was once told

Convenient to the set norms
A kid was lost, a kid was born

Confused between right and wrong
Swinging between weak and strong
All to become its future mature form

'Look at the way she talks'
She is not like the girls of her age
'Look at the way he cries'
He is not like the boys of his age
Or of any age, to be truthful

The kid who became too wise to be a kid
Is now too good to be true
The world for it is like fusion food
Sometimes tasteless sometimes good
The recipes are one well-kept secret
Every time different, every time new

I overheard them the other day
Broken syllables felt like a harp
One complained about repeating mistakes
Others said something about being all the same
All had something to say but nothing to do
It was like listening to a baboon venting like a
fool

I guess they were adults
They sounded wise
I don't think they will do something
For, I heard one of them shout
"This doesn't concern you,
you are not even that old"

But then what do I know
Am just a kid, either too mature
Or not mature enough
Whatever they say to stick the bluff

Am a kid to them when I don't abide
Am not one, when I start up a fight
A fight to pursue my dreams
A fight to question the Supremes

Only if they let me be
To carve my way and live free
Only if they didn't rush me

To move on to the next, even before I had taken
the first step
Only if they let me loose
To love, care, and find my faith
Only if they understood
That I was not theirs to save
But to comfort while I get slayed

"You must respect elders"
A kid was once told
"You must neither question nor answer back,
you must only know to follow"
A kid was once told

You must, you must not
You are, you are not
You you you
You, listen to me now

A kid was once told
When it was born
"It will become what we couldn't"
And why not, they made it
Now it must walk as they please

And thus, a kid was once killed
Falling for everything told in the name of love
It didn't stand a chance
To all the self-kindled irrationally rational tricks!

# Dust or Stardust

She woke up in a fiery heist
In the middle of a fantasy that everyone desires
A fantasy most deny to fancy

Thus, to a new but not so fresh morning, she
woke up
Last night was something of a fairytale
Of what she desired to be their truth forever
For every single moment was cherished beyond
reality

Amidst the droplets of passion
Her forehead burnt
Constantly hammering in the pain dripped in
disguise
The disguise she held so tight
That her very self was now someone else
Someone she was okay with, a friendly parasite

Dreams of her, felt like a century old
All taking a form that she admired
Admired in the moment
For what she had become felt like an
improvement
And why not, she had traveled too far

Traveled to terrains unknown
Trailed behind tracks turning sore
Wandering, hiding the explorer within
Or perhaps lost after all

All that she has seen
Sights I hear wish no one sees
Whites turning red
Reds turning Black
Black, so dark turning the kindle into a
farfetched possibility

Yet the fantasy desired
She had it all
She had what others dreamt of
Dreams of her own floating in distant skies
Ran down by waters unnamed
Pushed far by mediators unmanned

But last night,
Last night was somewhat of a dream
A dream like reality, coming to life
Life that she reached out to
Reaching out made it puff in clouds
Clouds of dust or stardust, hope or despair

All followed but none accompanied
Left everyone did not
Stayed some, yes, they did

But extending hands, she stopped
For fear kills more than death does
And feared she did
Feared of reality turning puff
Puff into clouds
Clouds of dust or stardust, hope or despair.

# Masquerade

I heard a story last night
She was dressed up all nice and bright
I was told that she knew
All that should have been new
Yet, she couldn't stay faithful to her knowledge
All she did was victimize the spoilage

One fine day wisdom surpassed her brains
She felt, this time this person wouldn't give her
stains
Wisdom was known to be the winner
Till this time, when it encountered its sinner

When both the pillars failed to serve her justice
She took everything for nothing, but a game of
chances
She felt, rather fooled herself into believing,
That there was nothing at stake
She had mastered the art to fake

Yet when she told me this story last night
She was dressed up all nice and bright
She was somewhat scared though
Feared not to reveal what went down
When facing the masquerades, succeeding the
crown

# This is not poetry

This is not poetry
This will not rhyme
Not even a fairytale
Maybe the one for you to say mine

One fine night
Beneath the star-studded sky
He was running helter-skelter
Looking for a mentor to shed out his banter
For he was lost
Lost in the mid of nowhere
Aren't we all too?

From seven in the morning
To somewhere around seven in the evening
Aren't we living someone else's life
And then end up saying
This is not how I pictured it to be

Anyways,
So, men ran helter-skelter in the middle of
nowhere
Looking for a light that would guide him in
despair

Wait! I see something, he says-
A light flashed; I think someone stared

Resumed, the chase continued
Expressionless, desperate yet detached
Looking for someone and something somewhere

Oh now I get it,
Somehow my eye missed it
The thing that glared
The eye that stared
All were a figment of my imagination
Because the one that was real
Was just me in lateral inversion

I told you; I warned you
This is not poetry
This is not supposed to rhyme
This is reality
Yours and mine
Harsh yet fine
All we have is ourselves
And yes, we must shine!

# What we call love

# Ode to my kindred spirit

I want to live with you
Sit with you, talk to you
Discuss all that disappears in nothingness
Breathe all that smells of wilderness

I want to dream with you
See this world through your eyes
Cuz baby you are magic
Shred by shred, thread by thread
All in all

I want to feel with you
The calm that surrounds you
The cloak that keeps you sane
I want a part of it
Baby I want a part of you

You are the mahogany scent
The feeling of home
I want to touch with you
All that's behind the shades
Together let's travel through the dark
I will be your light
You be mine

I want to taste with you
The joy of being alive
Drink all that's divine
Cuz baby I will walk all the way to see you
To be with you

So come here take my hand
Let's elope
To live together in a land far away
Cuz baby I am already living with you
In a parallel paradigm!

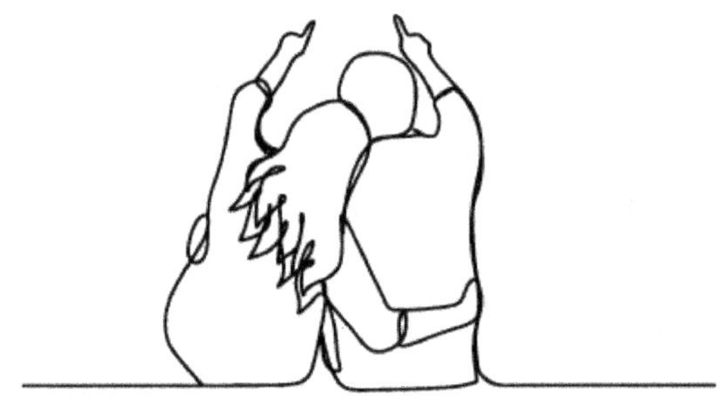

# Father of a daughter

For all those who know and for all those who are
They would second me on this
That it takes a bit more to be the father of a
daughter
No offense to the other half here
But it does take more sleepless nights
To raise a princess than a knight

Everyone says that the one who danced on my
birth was no one but my dad
I don't know but I'm sure
Danced or not, the day I was born it wasn't only
me who took a real form
There was this man who held me in his hands
Felt the warmth of my breath and the softness of
my little fingers
Who admired every inch of my existence
For he just knew he was holding a little bird in
her nest
"She is mine to take care of
She is mine to nurture hope", he would say to
himself

I used to pee in my bed when I was small
Everyone says he would shift me to the dry and
sleep in the wet himself

I wouldn't know if he did that or not
But one thing I know for sure
Since the time I remember and in the memories I
hold
There wasn't a single day when my cheeks were
wet or even in the summer nights I sweat
He used to sit all night and fan the demons away
For a good night's sleep was for her angel to
take away

I used to break things when I got angry
Everyone says that my dad never scolded me,
that he spoiled me
Spoiled or not that's for no one to decide
What's spoiled for you might be gutsy for me
But there's this thing, that only I know
The words of wisdom that came from him
Not to show that he was right, and I was wrong
But to be my torch bearer in times of darkness

I have a habit of falling at every tiny pebble I
step on
He never tried to remove those pebbles from my
way
He let me fall
He let me get hurt
He cried with me too
But those scars are the best teachings I have

To remind me till eternity, not to fall for the
wrong ones

Today when I look at him,
I see some things have changed
The face that used to beam up with a
never-ending smile on seeing his child
That smile, it's still there
But that face has more wrinkles than the spark it
used to have
Those arms that used to be my favorite set of
pillows (they still are)
They have grown weak
He has grown lean
That mustache, that pricked me whenever he
used to kiss me goodnight
It has turned gray
The man who always stood by my side as my
support system
Is still there, it's just that the fellow has aged

Don't worry dad, am here, we are here
To be your support system now
To make an attempt equal to at least one-tenth
maybe,
But yes I just want to say that I'm here to stay!

# A showstopper all new

Met this world as a little princess
To see her laugh was all priceless
She was always held tight
Never ever left out of sight

Step by step she grew
She was becoming more independent they knew
Family became friends, friends became family
Everything was moving seamlessly

Then one day something happened
Suddenly she felt all strengthened
It came to her that he was her prince charming
Childhood fairytales of whom used to be all
warming

Happy and blessed she took her vows
Wow! she got a new house
With some tears and one big smile
What she lived was now all back a mile

Took a rebirth she did
With a small difference that hid
This time a host of memories she had
Of the past life she led

Knowing a whole new set of people was a gift
For every relation she was to make a shift
She took all up
Handled the hub

Now at a brink
Her life once again is about to change in a blink
There she sits
Holding a little princess, yes it fits
The skit was set on a replay she knew
In her lap she had a showstopper all new (:

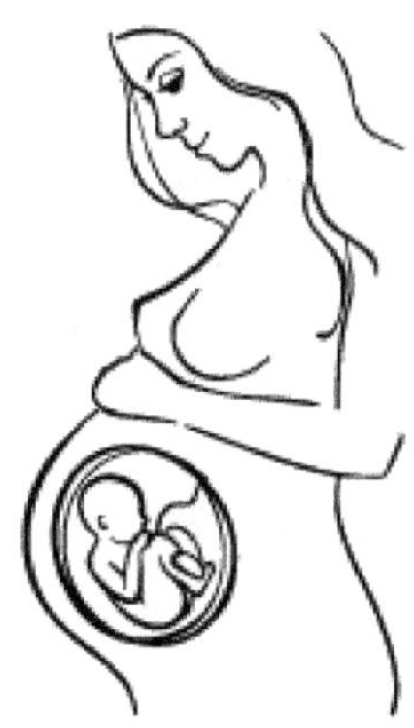

# The working Mom - An unspoken tale of love

For once she snoozed off
Then startled she woke up
It was half past six
She didn't want to get late

Skipped her morning routine
Rubbed her eyes,
Straight for the breakfast she went
It was presentation day

Running and panting
Neither a minute less nor a minute more
Straight to the bath she went
Sipping her tea she took her car keys

Halfway through
She received a call, it was an emergency
She had to call in sick

Headed back home
Picked up the file
Straight to the school she headed
And just like that, a long-awaited opportunity
Ran down the drains

She was still all bright and smiling
Her child hugged her
"Thank-you so much mom for bringing this to
me
I don't know what I would do without you!
Did I mess up with your office much?"
She hugged him back, "No son never"

And there it went,
All unmentioned once again!

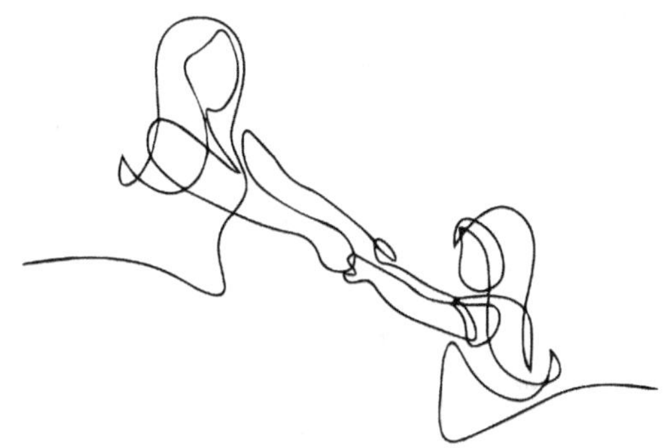

# Dreamy day

Clock is ticking
Wind is tickling
Once again, the world is singing

Oh, wait I hear a ringing
The day is calling
"Hey, how are you?
I am here again
Are you ready for the toiling?"

I wake up from my dreamy sleep
Rubbing my eyes, running my fingers through
my hair
"Hell, yeah am ready bring on the shaking"

I decide the day is bright and sunny
Stepped outside all ready and shiny
Before I know, it starts raining
You gotta be kidding me!

It's raining like heaven falls
And yes, yet again am running late for my
meetings
I pause for a minute and take a deep breath
Oh, that smell, I can feel the earth inside

I look around and decide
Well, it's not that bad
My clothes aren't ruined much
I still have my liner intact
My kajal not so smudged
I look pretty presentable in fact

So, I head with a beaming smile
Trembled down the steps a bit
And now I got a coffee stain
Perhaps it is not that a good morning after all

And as I am about to tag it down already
I see him walking towards me
Oh my! That's some serious gym time you see
Brown eyes, that flattering smile
I fell in love yet again as I saw him

I wish he was real though
For my celebrity crush just refuses to show up in
reality

Somewhat stumbling through the day
I don't know what's making me stay
The night is approaching
Am ready again to enter my dreamy world
Where reality will once again become fiction
And fiction will be the only thing that's real (:

# Remembering

You will say some stuff
And then you will say some more
Let me warn you here
I do hear
But a lot less would stay clear

There's a filter to my receptions
All that's not worth the substance, won't stay
I might ask you to repeat what you just said
Or would end up blank-faced when you refer to
a fact past said

You see I'm bad with dates
Birthdays and anniversaries for me are too
overrated
I might not remember the color of your shirt or
the specifics of your dress
But the heart would still malfunction the same
way it did on seeing you the other day

I might lose at those question games of how well
I know you
I don't know
If knowing your favorite color is more important
Than remembering what gets that pink tint on
your skin

You would accuse me of framing excuses
To stay clear of the dreadful shots
I agree, you are the one "more sane" still
Talking about real stuff had multiplied the
insanity quotient in me after all!

# Love

Once you were not there anymore
You became my muse
If I ever come back to you
I will make sure I am worthy of you

Why is it that the smallest of memories
Send me onto the biggest of spirals?

I know I wanted you to move on,
But seeing you attempt at it,
Kills me one moment at a time

I could throw out all the notes and letters
But how do I get rid of the imprint that you left
on me?

Your love was so kind and pure
That I don't even know if it was love
Because they said love was supposed to give
you butterflies
But you,
You gave me fireflies

I wish you light a million lives through their
darkest days
More than that I wish for you to find your sun

So, you can still shine bright on your darkest nights

# The game of love

Smile she did every now and then
Tease her; he did at every possible instance

Dreams were all she had in her shell
She was a little mermaid, she thought for herself

His world was normal until she happened, and
then
It never mattered how long was the distance

She occurred to him as a jewel
He didn't know that he was the jeweler himself

Everything was working as per the plan
Lush feelings they had immense

The other supported when one fell
Their aura pronounced what's amidst, itself

One day something felt kind of missing
They knew times were destined to descend

For here is heaven and here is hell
Love is a game mastered by oneself

# Love poem

You ask me to write a love poem
But how can I write about something am not
sure of

I don't know if I have ever loved or been loved
For all those gestures that we call for,
in the name of love
Aren't they some form of obligation?

If to love someone is to have them live and die
for you
Then how can love be selfless?

If to love someone gives you the right to hold
them accountable for your own grief
Then how is love the name of giving?

You ask me to write a love poem
But how can I write one

When all I know is to sacrifice in the name of
love
To live in the service of the other
To forget about your own desires

If getting married is the act of announcing your
love to the world
Then why do people fall apart?

If love forever and one true love are mere
expressions
Then, in the name of love, why do we
romanticize a happily ever after?

You ask me to write a love poem
And I will write one
The day we stop selling love wrapped in
chocolate boxes and red roses

I will write a love poem
The day love stops being a bargain chip
I will write a love poem
The day love calls for acceptance and not
expectance

I will write a love poem
The day two people madly in love
Stop trying to change one another
I will write a love poem
The day I see love move from reel to real life

I will write a love poem
The day love stops coming with an asterisk*

# Solving the Ys for my X

The day you left me
This world made me mark you
They said you were my X now
That no matter what
I should not go looking for you
That our equation was never supposed to
balance
And I should stop devising new methods to
solve it for you

Today...
It's been a while
It's been a while, but I still sometimes wonder
Y didn't we work out
When all I ever wanted was to untangle you
Y couldn't we solve our problems
When all you ever wanted was to brush them
under
Y were we unsuccessful in discovering the
unknown
When all we ever wanted was to hide from one
another all that hurt

Maybe, we were trying to equate the LHS with
RHS

And hence prove to the world that we were in
fact identical
I wonder if our hypothesis was broken, to begin
with
I think we were not meant to equate each other
I think, in the race of reaching the finish line
with a consensus
We canceled out on our constants
We kept trying to solve for a unique solution
When all we were, was just one possibility from
an infinite set

I do wish for you to find your constant
As much as I wish for me to find mine
And in the meanwhile, let's hold on to our Xs
and Ys
Cuz even if they did not hold up forever
They did keep the equation alive through the
hustle (:

# I Wonder

Do you ever wonder
After all this time
The person who once decorated your life
What would they be doing now?

What does their day look like?
What thoughts lull them to sleep every night?
Or perhaps keep them awake still

Do you ever wonder
Because I do
I walk by the place that we once called home
And wonder where you are now
I wonder if perhaps
You have a new home
Or in someone have you found an escape

I don't intend to
But I still sometimes wonder
The things that we used to do together
Do you still enjoy them?
Do you still forget to comb your hair?
And yet care a great deal about them

If this reaches you somehow
Don't worry

I am over you
I have been for some time now

It's just that I have a funny memory
You ask what I did today
I would probably fumble and stumble on a
couple of maybes

But then if you bring back the most mundane of
days
And a boring normal task
I would probably remember everything
From the color of your shirt
To the smirk on your face
Your unruly hair and the feeling of your
presence
For it was in those everyday mundane things
That we lived

Love did find us on the way
And it may be lost for the world
But sometimes on some days
I wonder

And suddenly it's all the same
By the whiff of a familiar perfume in passing
Or a voice resembling yours
I am taken back for a few moments
Until I shake it off to think

If you ever wonder at all?

# I before XYZ

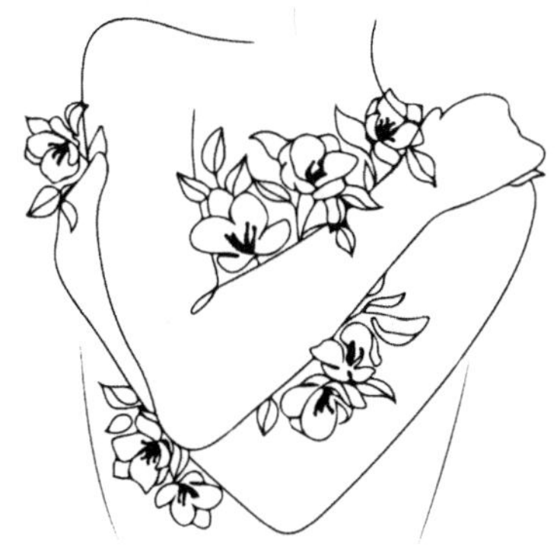

# Love or lust

When you say you love me
Am not sure anymore
If that's what you mean
Or with me, you just like to get seen?

I know it's not always easy for me to reach the
climax
But are you really interested in the facts?
There's more to me than you see
Within me there lies an urge to just be
I am not the deep brown eyes, the long black
hair or the sturdy specs on me
Though there's hardly anything else that I set for
you to peep

Is it something about me
That makes me worth the flesh you eat
Or is it just who you are?

Sadly, it's today when you are on my screen
Live as I caught you
With the one standing by your side
Feeling every inch of uneasiness that it reaps
For that's exactly where I want to be

But now I am here,
With a painting all over me
That am nothing more than a loaf
The side you endure with the main course

I don't want you to see me and think
That's the ugly secret of which I shall never
speak
I want to be the love that you are not afraid to be
with
I want to be the one you show off and not
squeak

# It's not about me, it's about you

It's not about me
It's about you
It's about the person I see in you
For when I look into the mirror
I am searching for you
As everyone left, you stayed
As everyone changed, you didn't

There's a singer silenced in you
A dancer paralyzed in you
An actor frightened in you
A painter color blinded in you
There's an artist lost in you

For there are a million dreams that died in you
Because the opportunist in you was dominant
always
Because the person in you couldn't see the
human in me
Still when your society didn't approve of my art,
my ways
You just didn't abandon me
You stayed

You stayed with a clause of not changing
yourself but me
And the opportunist in you slowly took over me
But you see,
It's not about me
It's about you
It's about the person I see in you
For when I look into the mirror
I am searching for you
As everyone left, you stayed
As everyone changed, you didn't

But there's one thing
If you are so loyal to make it a point to stay
always
Do me a favor and keep the writer inspired, the
traveler alive
Don't let them die
Can you do that for me?
Because if you take care of that
I promise it will take care of everything else
And I promise to take care of you

Because it's not about me
It's about you
It's about the person I see in you
For when I look into the mirror, am searching
for you
As everyone left, you stayed

As everyone changed, you didn't

Today as I say this to my reflection in the mirror
I don't mean to hurt you
I don't mean to pull a taunt at you
I only mean to praise you for your loyalty
Because you stayed

Even if it was the role of a kidnapper that you
played
To trap my soul and let it feed on the crumbs of
your leftover
I praise you
Because I know it wasn't your wish to treat me
like that
Even you were trapped under the "righteous"
web

I praise you, as you know
It's not about me
It's about you
It's about the person I see in you
For when I look into the mirror, am searching
for you
When everyone left, you stayed
When everyone changed, you didn't!

# Women

Don't celebrate me because I'm a woman
Celebrate me because I'm here
Celebrate me because I'm smiling after all that I
endure
You may say things are better than before
But it's not a halfhearted consolation prize that
I'm looking for

Celebrate me because I show up
I am not scared of a fight
I don't stand down when I'm right
Celebrate me because I love with passion
And lead with compassion

Celebrate me for I'm kind to others
And one of a kind in millions
Celebrate me for my uniqueness
Celebrate me for my flaws
Because oh my my
How flawed am I
I mess up more than I let on
I stumble more than I dust off

So celebrate me for the installments of pain I
endure

And yet brave a smile so it won't be too
uncomfortable for you all

I am not heavenly
I am not a Goddess
I am human and if you must celebrate me
Celebrate the never dying spirit I embody

Celebrate me by supporting me
By helping me do the daily chores
By making a cup of tea on a day when it's too
much to endure
Celebrate me by being there for me
By comforting me in times when I can't
necessarily hold myself up

And if you must celebrate me
Then celebrate me for my presence
Because you are aware that my absence would
be a great loss

Celebrate me if you think I am worth celebrating
for
Celebrate me if am worth waiting for

Don't celebrate me because am a women
Celebrate me because I'm a human, I'm here,
and I matter!

# I have a dream

I had a dream last night
A little clear and somewhat blurred seemed the sight,

It was all covered in a deep green hue
There in the middle I was holding a bru,

Rays of light peeped in, to form a spotlight
I suppose I wore a dress all white,

Sitting on a rocking chair with one empty beside
Someone sat there or not, it's yet to decide,

Sheets of some sort were scattered on the table kept in front
It displayed a visual that every now and then is burnt,

I lived in a woodhouse it seemed
There stood a jeep all black that beamed,

I lived in my dream last night
It all seemed real, and it might,

Some was ambiguous and I love it
It gave me a purpose to make sure that I
experience it,

I could feel the ultimate solace even in my sleep
Heaven if it exists, could not seep in more deep
(:

# Thoughts

To the thoughts that stuck around
I want to say "Thank You"

You make me who I am
You are, and hence we rhyme

I think about you and then think some more
One after the other, we weave what's in store

We have been on so many journeys together and
still are
I have seen you waver
And you have taken me to depths, oh so far

If you didn't decide to stay
How would I ever know myself
Word by word, piece by piece
We built what's uniquely ours

Now I say I know my words
Oh, it's so true, I owe you all the covers

I know I have cursed you a lot
When others said I overthink
I blamed you
For I didn't know any better

Now that I do
I have figured

You are who I am
You are the very reason of my existence
You are my root
You are my flight
You are what makes it just "All right"

Thank you for being a forever part of me
Thank you for lighting up the spark for so many
poetries
And lest I forget
Thank you… for helping me find the true "Me"!

# Why do I write?

I often get asked
Why do you write?
I don't know what to tell you
So then, I ask myself
Why do I write?
And instead of getting an answer
Guess what I do?
I write!

I write about how I felt when I first wrote
How I felt the most seen in my writings
How with every note, every single syllable I
untangle something within
I write about where I come from
And where I am headed to
I write about me and you
I write about the mundane things of everyday
routine
The coffee beans and the raindrops
The love and the heartbreaks
I write to clear my headspace
I write to share
To spread the charm of old golden days
I write poems and letters
To deliver a smile on your face (:

"That's all good, but I still don't know why do
you write!
You can simply talk instead…"

I will tell you what
I would do that
But what's love without a touch of romance?
For when I write, I flirt
I flirt with my thoughts, and I tease the paper
I smile when I feel it all flow out of me

You see, I create
I create to leave a mark in the space
I add a little bit of hope everyday

"Hmm… So then you write to tell your story,
you say?"

Well to be true, I am the one who started writing
But I think my writing will write me a beautiful
end verse
Something so splendid
That the next time you ask me,
Why do you write?
I will tell you…
But wait, first let me write something today!